nature's friends

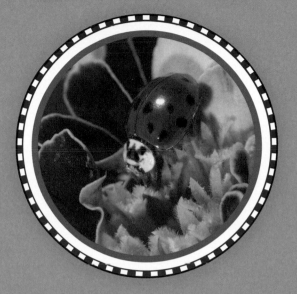

Ladybugs

by Ann Heinrichs

Content Adviser: Janann Jenner, Ph.D.

Science Adviser: Terrence E. Young Jr., M.Ed., M.L.S., Jefferson Parish (La.) Public Schools

Reading Adviser: Dr. Linda D. Labbo, Department of Reading Education, College of Education, The University of Georgia

COMPASS POINT BOOKS

MINNEAPOLIS, MINNESOTA

Compass Point Books
3722 West 50th Street, #115
Minneapolis, MN 55410

Visit Compass Point Books on the Internet at *www.compasspointbooks.com*
or e-mail your request to *custserv@compasspointbooks.com*

Photographs ©: Dwight R. Kuhn, cover, 1, 12–13; Robert McCaw, 4, 27; Anthony Mercieca/Photophile, 6–7; James P. Rowan, 8–9, 20–21; Bill Beatty/Visuals Unlimited, 10–11; Bill Beatty, 14–15, 16–17; J. R. Baker, N. C. State University, 18–19; ERIM, 22 (insert); NASA, 22–23; Philip James Corwin/Corbis, 24.

Editors: E. Russell Primm and Emily J. Dolbear
Photo Researchers: Svetlana Zhurkina and Jo Miller
Photo Selector: Linda S. Koutris
Designer: The Design Lab

Library of Congress Cataloging-in-Publication Data

Heinrichs, Ann.
    Ladybugs / by Ann Heinrichs.
      p. cm. — (Nature's friends)
    Includes bibliographical references (p.   ).
    Summary: Introduces distinguishing characteristics, life cycles, and different types of ladybugs.
    ISBN 0-7565-0167-9 (hardcover)
    1. Ladybugs—Juvenile literature. [1. Ladybugs.] I. Title. II. Series: Heinrichs, Ann. Nature's friends.
    QL596.C65 H45 2002
    595.76'9—dc21   2001004974

Printed in the United States of America.

Table of Contents

We Love Ladybugs!

Ladybug, ladybug, fly away home.
Your house is on fire and your children are gone.

Children all over the world know this poem. Ladybugs are one of our most loved insects. They eat bugs that harm our gardens and trees.

Children are good friends to ladybugs. In the United States, ladybugs are the state insect in seven states. Letters from schoolchildren helped make this happen.

◀ *Ladybugs are helpful in the garden.*

The Body of a Ladybug

A ladybug's body has three main parts—the head, the **thorax,** and the abdomen. The head has two eyes and a mouth. On top of its head, a ladybug has two antennae, or feelers. Ladybugs use their feelers to smell.

The thorax is the ladybug's middle part. It has six legs and four wings. Two of the wings are hard. They are the colored, spotted part you see. Under these wings are two thin wings for flying.

The abdomen is the ladybug's back part. It holds the stomach and egg-laying parts.

A ladybug's body has three parts. ▶

Kinds of Ladybugs

Ladybugs are also called ladybirds or lady beetles. They live almost everywhere in the world. The United States has more than 450 kinds of ladybugs.

Ladybugs come in many pretty colors. We often see orange ladybugs with black spots. But ladybugs can also be red or yellow. Some are gray, black, blue, or even pink! Some ladybugs have as many as twenty-four spots. Others have no spots at all.

◀ *Some ladybugs don't have any spots!*

Girl and Boy Ladybugs

"Ladybug" sounds like a female name. But there is no "gentleman bug." All ladybugs, male or female, are called ladybugs.

Female ladybugs lay eggs on plant leaves or stems. Babies called **larvae** hatch out of these eggs. Each larva changes to a **pupa.** It sticks to a leaf and goes through changes. One day a lovely adult ladybug comes out!

Ladybug larvae on a leaf ▶

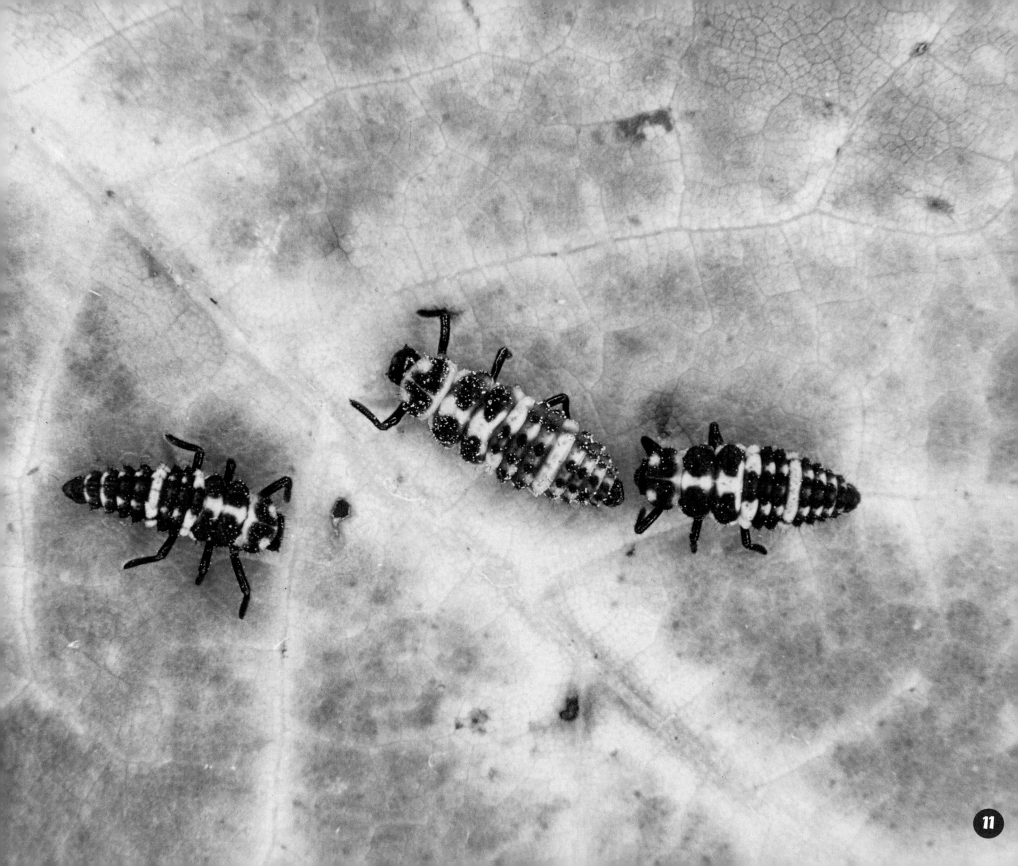

What Ladybugs Eat

People love to have ladybugs around their gardens. They are helpful insects. A ladybug's favorite meals are **aphids** and **mites.** These insects harm garden plants and trees.

In one day, a ladybug larva eats about twenty-five aphids. An adult ladybug can eat more than fifty aphids a day. In its lifetime, a ladybug may eat 5,000 aphids!

◀ *A ladybug eats an aphid.*

Wintertime for Ladybugs

When winter comes, ladybugs hibernate. This means they sleep all winter.

Ladybugs look for a warm place to hibernate. They may huddle in groups under logs or rocks. They do not need food in the winter. Instead, they live off the fat in their bodies.

You may find a ladybug in your house this winter. It probably came inside to hibernate.

Ladybugs hibernate under the floor in a house. ▶

Ladybugs in Danger

Ladybugs have to watch out for birds. Some kinds of birds are ladybugs' natural enemies. They like to eat ladybugs.

When they are in danger, ladybugs may simply fly away. Sometimes they "play dead" to fool an enemy. Sometimes they squirt out a yellow liquid. This liquid is ladybug blood. The ladybugs hope it will scare an enemy away.

◀ *A ladybug plays dead to avoid an enemy.*

Ladybugs Save the Day!

Ladybugs became big heroes in California in the 1880s. Orange-tree growers were in trouble. Harmful insect pests were killing their orange trees.

Ladybugs called Vedalia lady beetles were shipped in from Australia. They wiped out the harmful insects and saved the orange trees. Today farmers often use ladybugs to control insect pests.

Vedalia lady beetle ▶

Asian Lady Beetles

In the 1980s, a new kind of ladybug came to the United States. It was the Asian lady beetle. Asian lady beetles have saved many trees. They eat insect pests that destroy forests.

Asian lady beetles sometimes bite, but the bite is not **poisonous.** You will not bleed if this lady beetle bites you. The bite usually comes as a big surprise. That's because most ladybugs do not bite.

◀ *An Asian lady beetle*

Ladybugs in Space

Two ladybugs rode the space shuttle into space in 1999. Scientists put them in a cage with aphids. They wanted to see if ladybugs could catch aphids in space.

In space, there is no gravity. This means the aphids could not jump away. As a result, the ladybugs won. They were still able to catch the aphids.

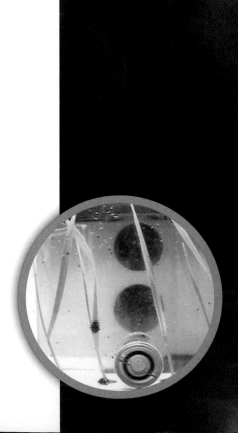

Ladybugs on the space shuttle ▶

Ladybugs in Your Home

Ladybugs do no harm in people's homes. They do not eat cloth or paper or plants.

You may find a ladybug in your home one day. If you do, you can gently take it outside. Or you can help it live inside. Ladybugs need water to live but warm houses are often dry. You can solve that problem by setting out a dish of water. In the spring, the ladybug will go away.

◀ *A young girl studies a ladybug.*

Ladybugs Are Good Friends

Ladybugs are good friends to humans. Even 500 years ago, people in Europe loved ladybugs. The ladybugs saved their crops.

Today, some people buy ladybugs to put in their gardens. Farmers buy them to protect their crops. Without ladybugs, aphids would kill rose bushes. Other insects would ruin crops, fruit trees, and forests. Ladybugs are great helpers and good friends!

A thirteen-spotted ladybug rests on a rose stalk. ▶

Glossary

aphids—very small insects that suck the juices from plants for food

larvae—the wormlike forms insects take after hatching from eggs
and before becoming pupae

mites—very tiny animals that are related to spiders

poisonous—containing poison that can cause harm

pupa—the form an insect takes after being a larva and before becoming
an adult

thorax—the middle part of an insect's body

Let's Look at Ladybugs

Class: Insecta
Order: Coleoptera
Family: Coccinellidae

Range: More than 4,000 kinds of ladybugs live on Earth. They live in many different places such as trees, shrubs, fields, and beaches. They may even live in our houses when the weather gets cold.

Life span: Average life span is two to three months, although ladybugs that hibernate through the winter live months longer.

Life stages: Female ladybugs lay eggs on the undersides of leaves. Ladybugs go through four life stages—egg, larva, pupa, and adult.

Food: Most ladybugs eat small insects. A few species are plant eaters. These ladybugs can damage crops such as beans, melons, and squash.

Did You Know?

Many people believe you will have good luck if you see a ladybug and you will have bad luck if you kill a ladybug.

Female ladybugs lay their eggs on the undersides of leaves to protect them from birds that might eat them.

The brightly colored and spotted back of a ladybug is really a pair of wing cases. They protect the transparent wings that ladybugs use to fly. When ladybugs want to fly, they open up their wing cases and spread their wings.

Ladybugs sometimes fly up to 100 miles (161 kilometers) to find food or a safe place to spend the winter.

Large groups of ladybugs often huddle together in a safe, warm place during the cold winter months.

Junior Entomologists

Entomologists are scientists who study insects. You can be an entomologist, too! Try to see how many kinds of ladybugs you can find. You will need an insect-catching net, a clean container with a cover, a notebook, and a pencil. Poke some small air holes in the cover of your container. Look for ladybugs near rose bushes, gardens, or fields. Sweep your net through an area being careful not to damage the plants. Place the ladybugs you catch in the container. Try to catch ten ladybugs. In your notebook, write down the color of each ladybug and the number of spots on its back. Handle the ladybugs gently and be sure to let them fly away when you're done.

Now try to answer these questions:
How many ladybugs did you observe?
Did all the ladybugs have the same number of spots?
Were all the spots in the same pattern on the ladybugs' backs or did each bug have a different pattern of spots?
Were all the ladybugs the same color?
How many legs did the ladybugs have?
How many different kinds of ladybug do you think you found?
How did you come up with this answer?
Draw a picture of each kind of ladybug you found.
Be sure to show its color and the correct number of spots.

Want to Know More?

AT THE LIBRARY

Coughlan, Cheryl. *Ladybugs.* Mankato, Minn.: Pebble Books, 1999.

Crewe, Sabrina. *The Ladybug.* Austin, Tex.: Raintree/Steck-Vaughn, 1997.

Hartley, Karen, and Chris MacRo. *Ladybug.* Chicago: Heinemann Library, 1998.

ON THE WEB

Lady Beetles

http://www.nysaes.cornell.edu/ent/biocontrol/predators/ladybintro.html

For more information about ladybugs and how they live

Ladybug Lore

http://claraweb.co.santa-clara.ca.us/parks/kidslbug.htm

For information about ladybugs in history and a short quiz

THROUGH THE MAIL

National Museum of Natural History
Office of Education
O. Orkin Insect Zoo
Constitution Avenue and 10th St., N.W.
Washington, DC 20560
202/357-2700

ON THE ROAD

Katydid Insect Museum
5060 W. Bethany Home Road
Glendale, AZ 85301
623/931-8718
To visit ladybugs and 2,500 other kinds of insects

The Philadelphia Insectarium
8046 Frankford Avenue
Philadelphia, PA 19136
215/338-3000
To see ladybugs and other insects in this all-bug museum

Index

About the Author: Ann Heinrichs grew up in Fort Smith, Arkansas. She began playing the piano at age three and thought she would grow up to be a pianist. Instead, she became a writer. Now she has written more than fifty books for children and young adults. Several of her books have won national awards. Ms. Heinrichs now lives in Chicago, Illinois. She enjoys martial arts and traveling to faraway countries.